BETWEEN SILENCE AND SILENCE

ACKNOWLEDGEMENTS

I am very grateful to Jeremy Poynting for his advice and help in bringing together and shaping this collection of poems. My wife, Mary, was always an inspiration and helped practically by typing the many versions of these poems as they emerged and changed.

IAN MCDONALD

BETWEEN SILENCE AND SILENCE

P E E P A L   T R E E

First published in Great Britain in 2003
Peepal Tree Press Ltd
17 King's Avenue
Leeds LS6 1QS
UK

ISBN 1 900715 37 6

CONTENTS

For my wife Mary and my sons Keith, Jamie and Darren

and my old friend Philip O'Meara

STILL...

Yes, it is as you say.
But let us get just one thing straight:
there is beauty in the world —
as when the hawk with sheathed wings
plummets in the morning air,
the child plays jumping in the ring,
the cloud-enshrouded sun descends in glory
in the river-mirror glowing
— yes, there is beauty in the world —
and the star-tree blossoms in the night,
night that will have an end.

I: IT PASSES

PRAISE SONG FOR MARY

Rounded
O of love
boon of heaven
heavy-looking now
birth soon to come
I celebrate the joy
beauty of body-swell
oval paradisal
proud miracle
I celebrate
all soft and circling forms
earth-root and flower
the golden pregnant moon
showers shadows
call-glory of carols
bowls of ripe oranges
rose mangoes full plums too
stuffed sweet melons
rotund sun-ball in the sky
fat cloud-bellies sailing
in looms and loops of light
smoke-mist over water
rain curves on river
ocean-swoops billows
roses pools of moon-water
home home home

Hollows look hallowed
they are the kin of hoops
fat loaves –
hot bounty
from old stoves
noontime and swallows

arcs of light
you are buoyant with becoming
a fountain
a meteor shower
flower-bloom
my burgeoning love
rock and cradling stars
in your belly-dark
time booms
and throbs and towers
life starts again
I hear the double-heart
that God made and me
and you will make me soon
a high-shining son

IT PASSES

Before the sun bursts upwards
pouring gold oil over the earth
darkness clings among the branches still.
In the quick-silver light
a humming-bird passes,
pierces bloom after bloom
for the hidden, cold syrup
clear as lit water.
Disturbed by the gleaming bird
flowers shiver down.
One gold petal falls shimmering
in a night-spun web:
quick, the spider glides to embrace
its gold and fluttering prey.
Thousands of years pass;
it happens again for me.
Murmuring, in the soft room,
my wife cradles a new-born child.
Night leaves behind a tender wind
like a song once heard.
I wish I did not have to die.

SHADOWS WILL HIDE THE SUN
(*For Darren, at the ceremony of baptism*)

Bathe him in light
I pray, bathe my son in light:
his be a good life's lustre.
Through a world growing dark
every passing hour
bathe him in light.
Let brightness gleam about him;
bitter will be days to come,
shadows will hide the sun.
Thus is the life of man,
but within him let brightness dwell.
Spare him dullness all his days,
defend him ever from despair.
From valley depths
let Heaven lead him;
never lose the mountain light.
Through gall and ash
a pearl will shine:
let his life gleam.
In the dark world
bathe him in light.

SMALL POEM FOR ALL FATHERS

To alarm their fathers half to death
new-born babies hold their breath
(mothers long by Nature schooled
rarely let themselves be fooled)
and gurgle when the jape succeeds:
attention is one of baby's needs.
By cavelight, since time began,
lumbering, lion-pelted man
bends to ensure his infant lives
(the babe, meanwhile, makes sure it gives
an imitation – and hides the grin –
of rigor mortis setting in),
bends lower still, in deep concern,
no sign of life he can discern,
'til bent as far as he can go
and frantic now to see life show
he jabs the baby in the side
to make quite sure it has not died,
and guiltily looks about
to see if anyone has found him out
in such foolishness, because, of course, he knows
the child is healthy as a budding rose.
And yet when night again descends
near baby's heart the father bends.
Despite himself he's never sure
whether baby's at death's accursed door,
through shadow stares and tries to see
on which side of eternity
the baby lingers. His panic grows
and grows, though well he knows
that babies are as tough as nails.

Night after night, it never fails:
he has to check the infant's breath:
sleep perhaps – but is it death?
So it has been since time began
and will be so until the end of man.

THAT MY SON BE KEPT SAFE

My small son burns with fever,
his whole body is furnace hot,
burning to death he seems.
'I'm so sick, Dad,' he'd said,
his eyes beseeching me to help.
Now his eyes are closed,
his dark lashes long like mine they say.
His breath rasps hard and dry;
it is agony to hear it.
To touch his brow stops the heart.
The doctor, stone-faced, stern-browed –
though we try to catch a saving glance –
will not look us in the eyes.
My wife, smoothing the bed, doing anything,
anything to help, to keep busy,
trembles with fear. I tremble equally.
It is the worst fear in the world,
fear of a sadness beyond all sadness:
God forbid this should befall.
All the years that pass
would not cancel out the hour.
Why are we constructed so?
were it not better to be a stone?

I remember times we watched him,
coming to his bed because we could not hear his breathing,
bending low and lower to catch the breath
just raising the small chest.
The slightest twitch of coverlet or ribbon
showing he was safe among the smothering pillows
was most sweet, most easing
of this fear we all have always
that they will die and leave us

No hope at all, the rest of life made senseless,
No ransom can ever meet this threat.

He burns to death
and my whole self cries to heaven.
For him to keep safe I would vow it now
to be good in God's sight always, always:
good father, good husband, good man,
Christ's good soldier even.
Though rum's still sweet
and friendship's fine, and laughter,
and a girl's walk catches the groin
and the world is so beautiful
and the wonder of every minute never ceases
I would give it all away forever
to let his eyes not close, my God,
that my son be kept safe.
And if God will not listen,
if God stops his ears,
so that my small son be saved,
I would make a pact
with the hobgoblin in Hell
who loves sudden misery,
who strikes when life is most fit,
to give all my gold,
give blood-health, body-tune, eyesight,
the touch of wind and water that I love,
memories I have of tenderest hours,
reason that controls all things
the life God gave me,
the immortal soul,
I would give all away
should my son be safe now:
safe now, my God, my God!

STAR OF LOVE

('At this time of the year in the early hours of the morning, Venus can be seen at its brightest in the Eastern sky.'
1988 Almanack: The Sky at Night for December)

My son cries out
and I am up to see him.
The sky is dark,
sea-wind blows in the rain;
there it blazes in the Eastern heavens,
the star of Love riding in the clouds alone,
gold ember burning tiger-bright.
Memory flies back
when I too was young:
my mother pointing
when I woke in tears,
voice gentle as a shepherd's flute:
'That is Christ's star,
star of love, my son.
It brings beauty to the earth,
blesses all of us.'
Now as I comfort him
I point again to the great star
blazing in the Eastern heavens;
my son looks in a wonder
that dries the tears in him.
And though the night is dark
and the hard rain blows in
my heart is filled again
with hope, the promise
that has lasted centuries.
'What is it?' my wife whispers,
our new child heavy in her.
'The Star of Love,' I say,
'The Christmas Star, my love.'

KITES, A TIGER FANG, A GOLDEN RING
(Silent's anagram is listen)

Morning broke clear across the sky,
water gleamed amidst the green glades.
A glorious chorus
of sweet birds sang.
I hugged my warm wife
and the children slept in safety.
Later we put up the kites
to sing in the high wind
across the sun.
With shouts of fear and excitement
the children found a tiger's fang
near the old engineer's tomb,
a giant tooth-claw on a bone.
I picked it up and told fearful tales
of the wild forest and the night.
When the stars appeared –
a black castle of such dazzling lights! –
my son and I sat under the sky
discussing mysteries.
Later, showering by lamplight,
my gold ring gleamed
– my grandmother's when I was young –
and I thought how it might end.
How long does gold last?
How long are rings kept?
Lost? Given to a careful son?
Sold if it comes to that?
Or on my bright bone still
in endless night?

WHITE CATHEDRALS

Five boys swim in the canal,
diving amid white lilies with golden hearts.
Water-shine gleams on their naked bodies,
eel-black beauty in the morning light.

No matter the weight
of the white cathedrals –
barns of heaven,
the massed shops full of goods,
the laugh-shatterers,
the exact and confident sciences,
the thud of marching feet,
nothing that the husked men say
can drown their joy.

SCORPION
(For Jamie)

Play in the sun, child,
play in the bright air,
run along the sweet wind
that has blown since time began.
Breathe the mango-scented air,
cast your kite into the high arching sky,
a brilliant bird upon the heavens.
Clasp me in your arms tight,
tight, until I feel the tears of joy.
Laugh, laugh in the glorious morning,
spin cartwheels on the grass,
shining somersaults of play;
in the kingdom of freedom take delight.
No time to warn you, no need:
the dry rustle in the dead leaves.

BEHIND THE RIB-CAGE LIES THE HEART

i

My six-year son is at my side
light-brown, glowing, olive-eyed,
he's precious beyond compare.
Certainly no gold or place of power
is worth hide or hair of him.
I would take unmeasured trouble
to keep him from a breaking heart.

Yet, unknowing, we cause agony.
He props a chin, intently reads,
then asks a question solemnly:
'Are bees made all of gold?
What is beeswax? Does it hurt?'
I make a tease of what he says,
throw the flowers in the flame.
His cheek tints rise in anger, shame,
he takes a swinging shot at me,
cracks me good and heavily
in my side, with all his force.
'Hey! young man! You're strong. That hurt.
You do not hurt the ones you love.
You broke my rib-cage right in two!'
That halts him most suddenly.
'Behind the rib-cage lies the heart,'
I tell it to him seriously.
The pale flash of a fearsome terror
wells up from his deepest being;
he confronts, alone, confused,
the mystery of a new-born word.
The wolf waits in the darkening wood
where spiders creep and prophesy.

'Please say I did not break it really.'
I laugh to put him at his ease,
show him what the rib-cage is;
he touches my still-beating heart.
I smile and tousle up his hair.
'Father, this is no laughing matter!'
I feel start up that timeless pain.
A great fool you are, I swear
I will not break his heart again.

ii Mountains of the Moon

Rapt in a book
about the desperate wars of men
I do not notice through the open window
the full moon rising
plump as a pumpkin;
golden calabash
pouring light across the heavens,
letting down its golden hair.
My son looks out in wonder
at the burning beauty of the night,
tugs my hand hard
to catch attention to this glory.
'Remember you said you love me
bigger than all the world,
all the rivers and huge forests –
all the tallest, most mighty things on earth,
the giant's palace built of gold.'
Grave and still, my hand caught tight,
he points, there, with a heart-rending wonder.
'Well, Dad, I love you too,
bigger than all the things you said,
far bigger. I love you more than anything,

bigger than all the seas and suns,
huger even than, you know what,
than the mountains of the moon!'
The moon rises in a perfect sky,
rides in all its mystery.
Nothing I can find to say.

MY SON SELECTS A STONE

When he was six and I was fifty-six
all that week-long holiday
my son brought stones from the sea.
What is this? A shark's tooth from the deep.
And these? Leaf of whitened coral.
Wave-worn bottle once held pirate rum.
Crystal from a drowned sailor's chain.
Magenta tile broken from a Great House floor,
a gleam of porcelain treasure-cup.
Snippet of glinting quartz we long pored over.
Are these valuable diamonds, Dad?
He lined them up to show his mother. Proud
cornucopia from the eternal sea. She praised him.

At the end he threw them all away,
kept none of the beautiful, the curious,
the sea-shaped wonders he had found
and brought for our appraisal,
but kept a solid, ordinary, small rock
no different from a scattered multitude
that I could see. He has it still.
He never told us why he kept it.

GREENEYES

By the green pool where the milk-bit cascadura is caught at morning
I meet my girl whose breasts have the scent of the sun-dried khuskhus grass.
I have nothing, greeneyes, better to say to you than this:
for me you are the last dimension in the touch of sense —
berry leaf, cocoa flower along its branch, white lilies near Easter River,
in them intricate as length and depth and colour,
as time they last, you are the binder of their form.
All my love you have brought them to the fullness of a season's rains
and now the balata tree has leaf falling to the stream-ferns
near this green and cascadura-haunted pool;
it is you who are its maker, meaner, who strips the tree to its diamond heart.
Come, greeneyes, feel the water like cold bracelets round your thighs.

BETROTHAL

Old story. Young girl getting bigger now:
fifteen, tender, good, submissive;
parents want the best for her:
pious, fierce for family and name,
and old traditions steeped in race and time.
Goldsmith's son is thirty-four:
had his days, boy, played an eager field,
wants to settle now and take a wife.
Offers house and future safe as gold,
cows and coconuts up Essequibo Coast.
The thing is done, families agree:
a marriage is arranged for all to see,
proud and suitable and good for all
except – she's irremediably locked in tears.
She will not talk to family or friends
except to say she does not wish to live
if this must be the burden of her days:
not furious but a quiet, downward look.

All are summoned against this stubbornness:
old, gentle uncles come, brothers hold her hands,
white-robed pandit shakes his head and warns.
They appeal to me: I see the girl
I knew since parents gave her birth.
She has her story when we sit alone.
Young man she saw once by the temple wall:
hardly speak though they meet at festivals.
Hands once touched, and held, and that's enough.
I say the sensible things I must
but eyes have blazed like that before,
storm-light on a sunless shore.
I meet my old, grey, saddened friends.
'She is young! What does she know of life!'

Yes, she is young as the new moon,
green as young grass after rain,
but what she now has is her heart –
hard as antique mountain stone
sleepless, ancient scythe of stars.
And, yes, she will kill herself
should you bring this goldsmith's son of yours.

WEDDING NIGHT

This cloudless night
stars crowd the sky,
a whirling bee-storm
glitters above the trees.
A table is alight with silver,
lustrous gifts presented
to shine with brilliant flowers.
The holy fire burns
amid murmuring of prayers.
Scarlet adorns her head,
sari of kindled flame.
Gold anklets shine on her feet
gold bracelets shine on her arms
a gold necklace gleams at her throat.
But brighter than all
burning with love
are her dark eyes
glowing in the lamplight.

II: MIDDLE AGE

MIDDLE AGE

i What Delighteth Me

A carnival of senses counted most:
it was drinking with the boys,
the marking down of women for pursuit
games of skill fought out on sunny courts,
the blaze of action in limbs or groin.
Tethered down at rest was like life lost,
passing time was ill spent with no company,
the itch of other people I had to scratch.
Candles guttering, dead flies in our wine-cups.

What a pleasure it is now
opening a new book I have wanted,
alone in a chair that fits my back,
anticipating delight, fingers cracking the pages,
the first sentences making the mind water,
no debts or business until tomorrow comes.
This is better than I ever thought:
pleasures quiet down, they simplify.

ii Dreams, Leave Me Alone

I am going along fine in the middle years.
I've left youth like a blazing fire
guttering out in albums, in old letters full of puzzles.
I am heavy with the stone of middle age,
the skin of all I touch is thickened,
a glaze on what I see,
sounds muffle like a pillow cuffed,
tastes fur like old peppers left in vinegar.
I smell the air; it has no smell at all.

I think the well-considered thoughts
that other men have thought before.
Unusual beauty I quite ignore or shun.
Like an old car on a cold morning,
I need a kick start.
But it's alright, lives find their level:
comfortable, not vivid, are the passing hours.
The joy of the world
is faded like a worn rug
in a sunny room.
It looks as if the time left
will be serviceable but not astonishing:
a walk, eyes down, through brilliant forests.

iii Tight Designer Jeans

The sun is shining and the girls are out,
walking two by two in full regalia
pretending not to notice what it's all about;
if men don't turn, reckon up a failure.
Breasts sun-silhouetted through silk-thin blouse:
the one intention is clearly to arouse.

From carnal prime observe a mighty fall!
I feel no prickling in the loins at all.
It is my middle age it seems.
This glorious girl in tight designer jeans
comes passing by in studied nonchalance
once I'd have grabbed at even half a chance.
Now no longer comes that yearning urge to watch
her sweetly grooved and clear dividing crotch.
Worse yet to 'fall in love' perhaps
and face the dreary, agonising lapse
into the unrewarding game of hot pursuit,
all because her perky breasts look cute!

Undoubtedly she sports a fine, upstanding bust,
but now I grudge the hours of such spectator lust,
imagining what might happen if one followed through –
and the worse waste by far if actually you do.
Count up the time, it fills one with dismay,
to think how many months and years are idly spent this way:
vast fractions of a lifetime absurdly spent
wistful, mindless, and concupiscent.

Asway they pass, I view the game with scorn.
Why does it hurt like this? They look at me and yawn.

iv Invitation to a Walk

The river gleams, the sun has burned all day.
'Come, take a walk and put your books away!'
I knew her kind, but she will never know –
such a girl, same sweet limbs, a long, long time ago.

So now I'll try my best, there's no one else to see,
but you and me, my soul, but you and me.
As life slides past, there's surely one relentless law:
getting old involves holding poses more.

Now confirmation comes how hard it is to lie
as looking out the corner of my slightly better eye
I try to make a judgment how she's judging me.
I force a virile-looking smile and leap up jauntily.

(Pretend for all you're worth the years have not departed
and feign a frantic sparkle now you've actually got started.)

Who said that youth, once gone, cannot return —
there's ways of seeming supple you can learn.
I ascertain my step looks full of spring —
bouncing on the toes is this man's thing.

There is an art in holding muscles tense
— the battle fought within is quite immense —
that makes the sag of stomach seem much less —
with care she'll never know my lungs' distress.

I flick away a longish curl of hair
which flops down, greying, out of place —
I well remember reading somewhere
such gestures hint a sort of awkward grace.

There is a knack of biting on the teeth
that sets the angle of the jaw just right
ensures the loosening jowls beneath
are not so unlustworthy to her sight.

There is a way of crinkling up the eyes
that makes the lines the years have scored
seem frank and humorous and wise
and not frustration's sad record.

I'm good at animated talk;
she doesn't need to talk at all —
there's quite sufficient in a young girl's walk
to hold such ancient flesh in thrall.

(The evening wind grows cold, I turn away.
I dream, I dream, and hurl my dreams away.)

My temper frays to see her youth.
Should I remind her of the truth:
beneath softest flesh the human bone
hides not even one erotic zone?

You miss a step, and catch my hands;
I see play-acting time is done.
My heart beats in forgotten lands
but you are only having fun.

Your flirting eyes cannot behold
my heart fill up with ageless pain.
In dreams my steps go striding as of old
and I am powerful and young again.

BREAD AND FISH HOOKS

A friend brought fat loaf-bread
crusty, straight from the oven;
I broke off a piece to eat,
taste of the first heat good.
He brought fish hooks, shining;
we followed a remote path, among stones,
dust gathering on our coats;
fished all day under a sulphur sky.
Returning, we ate a few small fish, roasted,
and the new bread he had given
and cold water from a plain jug.
We talked about the sea,
of other things too, like love,
but mostly about the sea which is large.
At night I had a vision of death:
a shore-line receding forever but always near
and a man walking there, gifts in his hands.

IRON POLE

The years wear all down.
Old men pass here
who were young,
strong and laughing,
walking on stone.

It tethered boats heavy with fish,
sea-wind, sea-wind,
blowing for fifty years,
rusts the iron pole
almost to nothing.

A remnant of it
juts from the stone sea-wall.
A fisher-boy,
fate-entangled,
stubs his toe
and his eyes are watering.

BURNING

Slowly, slowly my father shuffles to his rest,
my strong father whom I hugged for strength.
He sighs and settles; I kiss his stubbled cheek.
'I try to shave but now it takes up so much time.'
He rests. I lean upon the window-frame
and contemplate the night come on.
Moon-shadow of an antique tree
shapes slowly on the grass outside.
A candle near me sharply flares.
Wing of moth has caught the flame.
He rests. I hear the reddened sea-grapes drop.
Time's fire consumes us all.
As of old I take his hand. It's different now.
It burns. Eyes fill with tears to feel his grip.
Stars start to burn across the sky.

SIGNALLING

'After parties, in those courting days
He brought me safely to my door.
I could not bear to let him go,
Your handsome father — my young man.
He could not bear to leave me there:
When he left he turned and turned —
I see the stars above his head —
And tears of love came in my eyes.
A mile or so away he lived
Through trees, a tall apartment house:
We had a pact: when he got in
He lit his lamp, the window glowed,
He waved for me his silk-white scarf.
Heart raced to see that signalling.
My son, I feel my heart beat fast.'

The stars have burned for sixty years
The white scarf disappeared in dust.
My mother holds my father's hand;
Old and frail, he sinks to rest.

BEAUCAILLOU

The wind blows my mother's thin grey hair;
she speaks of Beaucaillou, her swift horse.
When she was a girl she recalls
the fine horse in his gleaming trap:
the snort and stamp and jingle
and her father laughing, clapping,
shouting, 'Home, Beaucaillou, home!'
And the wind blowing in her red, wild hair.

Most life is ice-melt,
bells through sea-mist,
dark coming home and hurrying.
There are no exceptions.
Thoughtful men feeling
the stars' pull across half the world,
knowing coasts' thick rocks
vanish in the seas' wash finally –
these men too have urgent private business:
they deal in golden things and lures.

Faded writing in a prayer-book's margin –
this remedy for love affairs and projects:
'Stand under old trees in the wind'.
Heaven is huge then and not temporary.

ON THE HEADLAND

Where I stand on the bare, stone headland —
strong winds scouring the sky,
white gulls floating, falling over the heaving water,
drinking in draughts of stone-cold air —
at the mouth of the great river,
the tide is turning, huge and heavy,
crashing on the land everywhere,
leaning on it, pushing, tearing, wearing it away.
The sea's salvage butts inland;
the big pieces grinding and rolling,
driven on the frothing face of waters.
I stand and feel I have not lived before
and will not live again to be like this,
where beauty, changing utterly to mystery,
cannot be understood or learned or justified.

Yesterday, in the village by the headland,
a man howled like a maddened dog,
broke the bones of his treasured wife.
It happened. I saw it.
A branch of flowers
shaking in the wind.

I feel the need to go from here, this stumbling place,
this stone and furious threshold to the world,
to find a welcome, the certainty of grace,
warmness, mercy, meaning; to turn the old,
true key of love so often used before
the flawless bolt that shuts the heavy door.

THE SAND-TRUCK DRIVER

I take the Seawall's pleasant air;
fishing boats come in, grey sails snapping
under a peaceful sky.
A sand-truck hurtles down the public road.
A small dog, crossing, begins to hurry up.
The sand-truck driver, crouched intently down,
swings the wheel fast, swerving for the animal,
follows it, fleeing, to the utmost edge of curb,
crushes the puppy into squealing pulp and blood:
an entrail-vivid mess scatters on the stone.
I cannot believe my eyes; briefly glimpsed,
the sand-truck driver's shoulders give a shake
and, head nodding in a sort of satisfaction,
he settles in his seat again, steers a steady course.
The fading day congeals and people hurry home.

What piled frustrations haunted him that day?
Wife's nagging, kids' snot-nosed monotone?
Something impossible in how he had to live?
Money nut-hard to get, proud strength diminishing,
failed shining children, bailiffs at the unowned door,
a sour general hopelessness daily to endure?
Or something deeper: sick of a sick society,
the feel of being hounded down by gathering circumstance,
No hint of wherewithal to give yourself a chance?

Or did, at home, that driver sip his tea,
the conversation with his wife so eminently sane,
dandle young Johnny gurgling on his knee?
Outside his window you may think you see
– of evil's lurking kingdom one glimpse may suffice –
smokestacks of the Central European plain,
the killing-fields of Pol Pot's paradise.

WE DO NOT STOP FOR STRANGERS

We were taking a comfortable ride
to a convivial party up the East Coast –
four friends talking boisterously,
laughing on Friday, relating office anecdotes.
A moon sometimes appeared between clouds
but mostly it was dark and the rain spattering.
A man appeared in the headlights waving,
Probably wanting a lift out of the night-rain.
He held a child by the other hand,
a serious small girl in a pink dress, barefoot.
I simply accelerated past the waving man;
right not to stop was the general verdict.
'Late already for the party, man.'
'You want to bet the child's a lure.'
'Pass back for you another time, old boy.'
Only later in the chattering crowd,
stuffing barbecued lamb, swilling rum,
I thought of this terrible conduct.
What has happened to me?
What has happened to the wide world?

FRAGMENTS

The piercing sense how good to be alive
brings home to us the culminating truth
life will be as good, but not for us
soon. We turn our aging eyes away.
The clear, bright Andromedean stars
emphasise the blackness of the void.
The more brilliantly a man's life burns
colder are the ashes that are left.

The night has been hot, restless:
far rumble of thunder, hardly heard,
reminder of incurable wounds.
Getting up and lying down again,
ache of bone beneath the flesh.
Even the fresh words of poetry pall.
Morning. A grey mist on the river.
The passing shriek of one white gull.

Peace settles here,
beauty rests.
Blaze of blue
over black water:
spurwings totter on lilies,
fish burst and gleam,
bamboos grieve and rustle.
Hibiscus flames
by the old tomb.
White lilies on emerald salvers,
water orchids purple as bruises
on anaconda-haunted pools.
Green flights of parrots,
rasping gargle of the howling monkeys,
click of beetles, whistling frogs.
Smell of wood-smoke,
lukanini cooking in a pan,
sweet guavas in the sun,
red mangoes rotting,
and centuries of leaves.
The rub of silk and mosses
liquid, thick sound –
gold dripping on stone.
Stir of alligators.
Silence, the silence of undiscovered noises.
A bolt of evening cloud glows red
like iron in a fire:
the sun-disc descends –
gold wafer down the throat of God.
The wind sighs;
old ghosts walk about:
a water-engineer and fisherman.
The dark pond crumples in a sudden breeze.

Silver ripples,
the wind in the throats of birds,
swamp grasses in the night wind.
Slim dark boats
slide past at midnight.
Where are they escaping?
Here is love, balance, ease,
context and perspective,
certainly in valuable things,
long, unflustered, thinking time,
a chance of choosing perfectly.

Morning comes –
suddenly a shining:
a bird skims down;
the silver surface breaks.
In life elsewhere the vital lies await.

Hours travelling
the dazzling river;
the black creek
is welcoming now;
shadows shivering cool,
tree-green overhanging.
Sudden as its scream
I look in a hawk's eye.
Young in a nest near,
it will not flinch
from the low branch.
Again, again the screech
its battle cry;
the hawk defies me.
Try gesture imperial
– Man is master of all –
fails, unmoves it.
Lustrous wings arise
in combat, not in flight,
even if it dies.
The inflexible beauty
stops me.
Icy agate eyes'
fire of anger and love
pierces me.
It was here before me,
that scream, that ancient eye.
Pass by.

AT THE CREATION

This is a place of arid, enclosed rock
where the storm's thunder is heard best,
cannoning and echoing, reverberating, rumbling,
rolling tremendously down the gulch-land
when clouds mount the heavens in black battlements.
Valleys, walled with hard, forbidding stone
high as eagles hanging on the sky,
hold bare shattered slate and ruined granite blocks.
A few trees stand in pools of dry earth,
stunted, hunched sideways by the wind
that whistles full of heat down narrow gullies.
Earth crumbles under the harsh beat of sun;
falls of rubble lie beneath these valley cliffs;
the sound of small, far avalanches
threaten and alert the wanderer.
There is no sign of man, nothing
man-made, man-handled, man-kept,
nothing soiled or greasy or disposable,
not even a carved rock or bright pennant in the wind
to show the history of man or man's mastery,
only the litter of wind, sun and beating rain
over ten thousand thousand years, and old debris
thrown out by the great earth shaking;
only the storm-shifting sentinels of stone,
crusty vomit of age succeeding age succeeding age.

Why have I climbed here utterly alone,
setting out from others with only water flask
and bread and a few plums in a back-bag,
without a watch to make a sound
or show that man has put a grip on nature?
It is not for wisdom that I venture here:
the bleak perfection, the empty, stone-filled scene,

adds not a thing to the mind's essential imagery.
It is not to trawl for beauty in this turbulent high air:
for me no beauty in what's so austerely stripped,
gaunt, burnt-out, dull, lustreless and bare.
Not for testing bravery I climb the stone-filled valley:
I am careful, steady, test each step I take
and others are not too far away for shouted help.
It is not to get an inkling of how saints feel
that I have come: such purity is quite beyond
a short, unpleasant walk in this mountain place.
It is not because it's there, that I have climbed:
that proud, ironic challenge was not meant for me.

Trouble in defining? Look close for sentiment:
it wells up an endless spring, a great torrent,
a teeming source of reams of inspiration,
agonies, ecstasies, incoherent, ill-expressed –
discipline flies weeping out the blood-red casement.
Fuelled by yearnings vague as hope and glory,
a dazzling summit beckons; we slither
on its slopes, struggle with the craft of poetry,
until dust brushed aside, clear rock, gold-gleaming,
shines under it and shines forever.

Such shaping of the formless stone beyond
the shadow fall may come once only,
may never come, a flash, a blast of light,
blood shot through Christ's shroud, at death,
who knows how. And we are there at last:
the reason why we climb
empty valleys filled with stone
and thunder from the sky.

SEEN THROUGH CLOSED EYES

Mountains hung with dreams;
from the caves, whispers of healing.
Across the onion field
bright berries glow in green trees,
flights of birds
soar below the thunderhead –
sudden circles of light.
Remember how love burns
before flesh and bone are parted.
Faraway, tipsy as Pharoahs,
children shriek with joy.
The noise of time fills my ears
endless as the air.
Fire-falls, the dying of the day,
and then the intensity of the night.

'Now death could come,' said one.
'Life has nothing left;
the hours are filled with pain.
Let sweet death come.'

'No,' said the other.
'If every century past
a bird wing brushed a stone
big as Hog Island
and death would not come
until the wing wore out the stone,
still death would be too soon,
still death would come too soon.'

RAIN

No rain for months, sky hard blue,
ground hardening like iron,
earth hot to shod feet,
smoke-shawls from bush-fires;
sun glares red before night falls.
White the worst colour, bright as bone.
Time soon coming when the oxen starve;
grass turns to ash, savannahs
send up clouds of burning dust.
Green is a colour gentle and forgotten
like blood gone from a dead face.
Mud cracks in pools once sweet with lilies.

Old men, who have known
the hard seasons, say
water would be the best gift
if it could be wrapped.

And so it comes, a fundamental beauty,
a simple thing not often counted –
like love; when it's there life balances,
though we do not feel the balancing,
until departure leaves us husked and dry.
It comes again and steadies us,
soothing, far away, a noise in the clouds,
a summoning freshness in everything.
An arid heartland springs alive;
water is love; it clears and shines:
clemency for a wracked land.

CHERRYBAGS

Rain in the marketplace,
black night falls,
glittering, dripping night.
I wander among the bags of red cherries.

Why did the world begin,
where will it end?
Books are written,
but nobody knows.

Only these three bags of cherries,
plump and rich,
stand in the market stall:
one bag leans to the side,
spills twelve red cherries.

A blackbird flies down,
beads-of-gold-eyed,
steals a red cherry;
red-pearl beaked,
proudly looks around.

It begins and ends,
balanced amidst the stars.

III: ARCHIVE

ARCHIVE

One by one the old men die:
the libraries are burning down.
On Lombard Street near Ma Belle's parlour
in a high and rotting house
greyed by time and fungus weather
I find one of the last ones,
a century old, and half alert.
He inhabits a bare, discarded room;
greets me sitting on a single bed.
A quarter candle gives him light;
enamel basins catch the rain.
The food is peppery, the rum is strong.

In a cracked mirror hung askew
I catch sight of my own lines of age.
The shadows carve them dark and deep:
shocked to think I'll follow him so fast.
Nothing keeps; the years defeat us all.
Framed in silver on the bedside table
a picture set to seize the eye:
Sunday dressed and stiffly posed
a small boy holds his father's hand.
When the city tidies up this life,
the silver frame but not the picture
is all that will remain of both.
Decades too late our heroes are acknowledged,
names announced in unattended stations.

Gnarled fingers like black twisted roots
now clutch an ancient bamboo flute.
He plays a twittering, faltering tune;
it peters out and leaves him sad:

'Oh lawd, brain get hard like bone!
Pickle to stone, pickle to stone!'
Stored in his memory are a thousand songs,
now and then he finds them still –
thumps his hand and shouts them out –
and stories for ten shelves of books,
gold chants, cures past numbering,
tinctures from the sap of plants,
lotions, balms from crushed green leaves.
He tells tall tales from Pomeroon:
charms, hunting signs, bull-monsters
from the dark forest, fires witches hung
from starry heavens, tribal flags, and waterfalls –
why they hacked the head off the bone-white ram…

But things are fading fast for him:
recalls exactly how the century turned,
he can't remember yesterday.
I take some notes. But it is sad.
Nobody keeps old bibles any more.
The old man sighs and shakes his head,
hums when he forgets the words.
The young men do not want to learn
and old men do not live forever.

MACARTHUR'S LIFE

What happen to old MacArthur
I wonder. They call he Barnyard
when he young, Slim Boy, Hot Cock.
All about town he run, crowing, mounting,
sunlight and morning, stain-sky and night.
It so sweet, why he should bother about anything else?
How a man like he could always find women?
He never pay but he always get. Something, boy,
something in this world; people don't want lonely.
But he get old and begin to fall in trenches.
Women ease he for a while, then drink.
Like he could always find women, he could always find drink.

He eye soft, people like he,
he never pick up a stone to pelt.
The years go by so quick, life waste, life done.
The last I see Slim Boy he look groggy
and like he trying something new, I don't know.
Mass finish at Sacred Heart, I see he in a pew
sink on the knee, head bend, one hand shaking.
But that was years ago; I don't know after.

Sing-Song work forty year in Parkview Club.
Everyone know Sing-Song; he rum-punch famous.
He humming happily when he make the drinks;
everyone know he style, he take good care.
He bother how much ice, perfect measure,
he proudly bring the drinks, as if it matter.
He like to hear compliment; it is he life you know.
He don't know nothing else, he don't want to know.
He share a lifetime with a God he love.
They come with slide-rule and computer, the new people.
Parkview Club change hands; they measuring money.
Sing-Song spilling a few drinks now, he old,
and how he could learn to put a pinch less
when he know the taste going change with that?
Better you put out light in he life.
So he have to go. They knock he off. Who sad?
Redundancy nothing much when dollar value gone.
Well, I hear they closing Parkview down:
computer working good, customer leaving fast.
Why they could never learn true cost?
Sing-Song take it easy, he humming still.
He gone by squatting fields to get a lot.
He build a shanty; it is Sing-Song Place.
Poor people also drink, now they have their prince.

CANTICLE OF THE MAIN STREET MADMAN

The old man blesses stones and men,
a supermarket clerk for years,
they say he has gone mad.
All day he signs the cross on things:
food, trees, earth, and the rubbish trucks.
He stands in Main Street blessing men.
He lifts his eyes towards the sun
blessing that great medallion too.
All night heaven's holy stars are blessed.
I've seen him bend down very low,
give benediction to a lump of shit.

He kneels in rainstorms, blesses them;
bliss lights his mild and streaming face.
Trench lilies red as blood he blesses;
he wades up to his waist in mud.
Birds! Takes a special joy in birds;
they perch or soar, he blesses them
with gestures wide that tell his love.
Stands by the churches during Mass
and signs the cross on celebrants.
Perhaps he means some irony;
he does the same thing at the banks.

What harm does this man do?
All he does is bless the world –
more sane than me or you.
They say he troubles normal men;
it interrupts the train of thought
of busy men, of serious men,
to have this peculiar man intrude
and sign the cross on their backsides.
Degrades the human race, they say.
Who will forgive our sanity?

The only men he will not bless
are policemen. They treat him rough,
come for him, 'Main Street disgrace',
cart him off like roadside rubbish,
bundle him into Brickdam station.
'Cool your blasted arse in there!'
But inside he starts again;
the four walls of his cell are blessed
and any inmates that are near.

He has never tired in his work –
must have blessed the whole of town.
Shakes with age now, soon will die.
Wonder who will take his place?
Who will bless us down the years?
Who will bless the men and stones?
No one will be mad enough to try.
Bless us, Lord, when he has gone.

THE MAN WHO TOOK THE PLACE OF GOD

Beyond the sea-endangered coast,
interior-deep, where rivers spring,
past white quartz outcrops shining in the sun,
green trees clinging on the steep slope downwards
to the burnished foot of the silver cliff,
trees, orchid-studded, swaying in the wind
the mountains make all day,
I visit the black doctor of the tribes –
'Protector from calamities', they call him.
Forty years have passed since he was rich in town,
his practice built with money-conscious skill –
society buzzed around his Brickdam home.
One day he packed a small bag, left,
aimed for the deep forest, met Potaro men,
never came out to the coast again.

He discovers herbs, cultivates his garden,
dreams brimming past the edge of time.
In a plum tree's shade he rests, swaying
in a swinging hammock, greets me with grace.
Light on the wind, hawks soar above us.
He speaks of the salves he makes,
the teas and ointments, bandages of leaves
to suck the bad blood out, root cultures,
aromatic balms, gut-soups of bark and buds
from plants no man before him ever saw.
His eyes are clear, his fingers rub an ancient stone,
cleansing aloes on a sour-wood plate.
'I've side-stepped death a thousand times.'
He keeps a room where spiders float,
spinning webs for wounds that tigers make.
The cracks in tortoise shells tell him of the future.
'They say, far off, there is a vine

wrapped around a solitary tree
four centuries old.
The vine has blossomed only once
and will blossom soon again.
Its fruit will make my old skin smooth.'
He shakes his head and laughs, ha-ha,
slaps his hands above his head.
'Tomorrow I will search for it:
I want to live forever and be young,
peach-skin shining, young as morning,
all my work to do.'

MR. PERFECTION

His name was actually that, Manuel Perfection.
The certificate in a slim dossier sets it out:
born in Bartica, Good Friday, nineteen twenty-four,
son of Theodore Perfection and his wife Mathilda.
Schooled by Catholics until the age of twelve –
'A bright boy but rebellious and does not love the Lord'.
Then he left 'to seek his fortune in the bush'.
Laconically a priest records the facts.
The vast forest swallows him for fifty years
and the time has passed like the wind
and the time has passed like a flying cloud
and candle-flies have winked ten times
and soon enough time brought him here.
He died this morning, not pleasantly,
a long time struggling to take a breath
until I, beside him, grew breathless too.

Before me rests the brown folder with his life.
Certificate of birth, baptism card, a school report, a letter.
That's all, except the page that ends the file –
sparse list of all he brought in here: bloodstone, knife,
old clothes, a cap; Matron countersigned the list.
The letter dated from thirty years ago,
dirty, scorched with fire, water-marked,
crumpled, it seems, once in an angry fist,
creased so many times it tore in half,
fixed, refixed, with transparent strips of tape.
I read the lines between the scorched-out parts,
guessing words but the sense is plain:
'You deserve the praise of this community
and its children most of all, who thank you.'
A village schoolmaster writes the thank-you note.
Such notes in thousands make up our lives

and some keep many and most keep none at all.
'You did the job well, all of us are pleased.
The desks and chairs you constructed to perfection.'
I'm sure that word was not deliberate —
the note looks hurried, there are words misspelt.

We all keep things whose value others miss,
shadows of hands that have caressed us.
This is what he culled and kept
and I will keep it too, to remember
how the wind changes and the centuries go
full of meanings we can never know.

A SIMPLE MAN

The garden needed more attention
we had decided. A man was at the gate,
slow-witted, surely; the first time that he spoke:
small vocabulary, stuttering words,
hesitating diction and a frightened look.
'Ah want the job. Ah could work mo' hard.'
A froth of spit lightly lined his lips.
What made us let him stay I do not know.
The routines explained, it took him long,
but gradually he learnt the daily rules
of cutting, clearing, digging, planting,
the right amount of watering, mould to be applied.
Learning all this slowly strengthened pride
and self-assurance grew as flowers bloomed
beneath his fingers, trees came to blossoming
and trellised vines shaded paths he cut.
A day came when he could take steps himself
to make more beautiful without instruction –
what he had begun and now had got to know
in his heart's root through utter dedication.
He just did small things very well –
repeated and repeated day by day by day
never letting his attentive eye divert,
not letting love withdraw at all from work,
until the year's end saw the good results:
a tended patch of earth transformed, green,
serenely ordered, shining with the fruits of care.

As the great plots of the world unfold
my thoughts drift often to this simple man.
There are few that catch the eye of history
and those that do, break the world or save it,
discover truths that none have found before,

find the fires that make the stories ring
and art shine for centuries, make timeless song.
All others born are lost beyond their deaths.
A man at peace who tries his best
and gives his share of love and work
but knows no dimension but the ordinary
is forgotten quickly in the seethe of time.

He has been with us for many peaceful years,
daily has he filled our lives with good.
We wake at mornings and hear the sounds of work,
the sweep of broom, earth being dug and placed,
water filling and the clean chop of wood,
the tuneless whistle which tells his peace of mind.
The house will fill with flowers and green leaves.
I know that this is good. It holds the sense
of work fulfilled and certainty and grace
enduring beyond the purposed hour.
It's said that nothing lasts,
but if what's good keeps,
then this, I know, will keep forever.

DEATH OF AN OLD WOMAN

She was eighty-five. Death came for her
without fuss, walked in quietly,
nodded to us all and took her hand
as if to say, 'Come now, it is time,
it will not be hard' – which she agreed
and lulled into the sleep that will not end.
She had been preparing, a quiet came on her,
and then she wanted one last thing:
the summoning of a son she had not seen
for many, many years and wanted now to hold,
touch his face, remembering where that scar runs,
how he fell and cut a child's brow fifty years before.
She waited for that, his summoning, his tears,
put up her frail arms to be embraced,
sighed and touched his face again.
Wanting nothing more, she closed her eyes
and welcomed patient Death, the comforter.

With pride she'd kept the small and spotless house
she and her husband owned for fifty years;
when he died she followed old routines
that he had known and she would not forget.
In their corner room that catches the sea-wind
each morning, she cleaned out floor and cupboards,
aired the clothes, made beds smooth and fresh,
then, as the sun rose, or rain perhaps swept in,
always she must spend time at her window-sill
breathing in sea-wind and the smell of pomegranates,
looking out on what was hers and, further out,
far sky spreading and the sea, on what was God's.
This morning scene she knew by heart and loved
as men love things they make, like bread in their
own homes, earth daily dug, chairs and tables

not moved for generations
and seasons' chores that children teach their children.

The morning of the day she came to die
she could not reach the window from her bed,
asked those who waited there to carry her
again to breathe the salt sea-wind, that
all those fifty years smelled gentle, sweet,
and come next sun rise would not feel again.

As the day wore on, silence lengthened
in the air, and she got clear of things.
At evening time when dark had not quite come
she died so soft one hardly knew,
and the stars shone brighter and the night went on.

She'd begged her sons that holy fire
should take her to eternal rest;
no dark and lonely earth should rot her bones,
or worms creep into flesh that once was sweet.
But fire! Fire she loved, the purity of fire.
'Entirely I am burned away,
I die and then I cease to die.'

She lay in white cloth, pure as light,
her white hair braided, limbs composed for sleep;
a husband-given bracelet from their courting days –
she loved this more than anything she owned –
hung on her fragile wrist, no other ornament
except clear lines of peace and beauty on her face.
Those she loved gathered where she lay,
they closed the casket at the last,
threw flowers in and fragrant herbs,
and heard the pandit speak the ancient words of hope:

'Life lasts a moment,
yet it does not end.
Even as a jewelled drop
returning to the sea
is this woman's life:
the sea is measurelessly deep;
even as a spark
from the great fire
is this woman's life:
the fire burns forever;
even as a single blossom
falling from the tree
is this woman's life:
the tree does not cease to bear.
Yesterday she was born,
tomorrow she is born again.
Entirely she is burned away;
the fire only mounts the higher.
If you shed tears
it is not for her they fall.
Does one sorrow for the boundless sea?
Does one sorrow for the great fire?
Does one sorrow for the blossoming tree?
Though darkness seems the lot of man,
all the universe is radiant light.'

We walked the enamelled fields of green –
ox-eyed flowers lined the way,
grasshoppers brushed against our feet –
and reached the place where she would burn
in brilliance in the flame she sought:
clear sky, oiled bier of wood, bright evening sun,
sea-wind to make the fire blaze and leap
heavenwards with the anointed soul.
There, on cleared ground, near the lapping waves,

we brought her, said the last farewells,
heaped aromatic wood around her like a house
where she would live a moment, bathed in fire,
until the flames consumed her utterly,
even the bones made ash as light as petals.
At the far corners of the holy bier
Pandit directed where the sons should set the fire.
Slowly it caught the oiled wood, coiled, and grew;
soon flames were tall and climbing clear,
bright pennants in the evening air.
For her no sinking in dark earth
but a leap lightwards, a resurrection
made of burning light, the deepest caverns
of her soul made marvellously bright.
For an hour the clear flames leaped and soared,
then sank to glowing red, a flower in the night.

The chosen son walked lonely to the wall
at morning's flush of pear-pink light,
gathered the ashes in a blessed white cloth.
Fishermen took them on this journey
under a sky now bathed again in light,
and then he cast the ashes wide upon
the sacred bosom of the sea, and threw
a solitary flower from the garden
she had loved so well, and watched
it float far, far upon wave succeeding wave
until it too was lost in blinding light.

HISTORY

History is
a drift of dust
the wind blows away
and forgets.
Gold and stone,
gossamer,
the mountains
of the setting moon,
Egypt's thrones,
old Aztec altars,
Rome's high tombs,
are dust.
Saints' blood dries,
empires end:
they are dust.
Walls that kept out
infinite armies:
a child steps softly
on the dust of them.
The horn of plenty
of love and art
lasts for a time,
is dust too at last.
Man's rights strong
as sacred marble,
the trumpets of justice,
are dust.
The grey walls of Auschwitz
are dust,
and the rose of mercy,
dust.

IV: THE BIRTH OF POETRY

SPINSTER GANTEAUME AND THE BIRTH OF POETRY

Close neighbour of the first home I knew,
gaunt spinster, Bernadette Ganteaume
('On the morrow God will rise again'),
I remember her always in long green dresses,
face bumpy with rosy unerupted boils.
Thick lenses made her pupils hugely bulge:
eternal gargoyle to a little boy.
Cats followed her and she was kind to them.
Lives like hers are blurs of memories like these,
except once – remembered like a bright wing
caught in ancient amber shining like the sun –
when poetry transfigured memory.

One dark night, she woke in fear;
drops, thick and slow, not water, fell on her.
With light she found them golden-red,
oozing spider-webs of gold, dripping
luscious oils from ceiling cracks,
bright honey from the dark attic of her house,
rain of strangeness smearing her white sheets –
generations old and proudly kept – embroidered
with the blood of night-birds in old heraldic tales,
pearls hanging from the open wounds of Saints.

She was a keeper-to-herself,
did not interfere with others' lives
nor wished others to interfere with hers.
But now, the sun just up with singing birds,
she fled her dark and golden house
and came to us to calm her heart,
to tell her story with dramatic hands.
A small boy sat and rubbed his eyes in wonder.
My father acted with concerned despatch.

Mid-morning the bee-catchers came sternly in;
children gathered round in awe
to watch heroic men in masks of black,
stiff yellow canvas suits and leather gloves –
like falconers playing with enormous hawks –
tramp bravely into old Ganteaume's tidy house,
ascend the dark attic to the golden hordes.
There they caught the Queen of the great honey-hive
that all the bright long days had built and burnished.
Then descended, with due ceremony –
to me, transfixed, it seemed with princely step –
casket before them, careful not to let it fall,
(memory tells me it was all of shining gold)
encrusted with golden bees at worship still,
that held the Queen in living, jewelled thrall.
The attic's abandoned bees they smoked to death
in black-winged thousands and swept them out in heaps.
For months old Ganteaume's house with strangeness shone,
fragrance drifting as from the caves of Gods.

A wheelbarrow came over to our house –
somewhere I still hear the axle creak –
filled with cakes of honey-comb,
dripping red, thick heavy drops.
I ate the crisply shining gift of cakes,
heaven's food, sweetness lacing the tongue.
Later huge stars came out in thousands,
seemed to fill the arching sky with light
golden rivers streaming in the night,
stretching without end, a pulsing beauty,
heaven's nearness blazing on the world.

What transmutes the ordinary to other,
as the host-bread baked by sweating men
becomes the living flesh of God?

Men transfixed by poetry,
what first transfixes them?
Memories of love, pain and mind's awakening,
the various beauties that overflow the years,
are not so strong for me as that attic full
of golden bees, the extraordinary honey-spill
the ropes of sweet, pearled honey-drops,
the bee-encrusted casket of the Queen,
a wheelbarrow arriving at our gate,
creaking, filled with honey-comb —
the golden hives that dripped on old Ganteaume.

AN OFFERING OF STONES

He got to know his only son,
He had just time enough for that.
In the small time he lived
he looked into his dark eyes,
he kissed his cheeks a hundred times.

A twelve-day lifetime,
all of it a struggle of breathing,
fists of such smallness, such delicacy,
desperately clasping, unclasping, clasping,
timed to each breath, rise and fall,
as if reaching, grasping, reaching,
grasping for the great gift
being slowly pulled away;
the gift given for twelve days,
and then no more.

Wandering along a stony way
he chose a few unusual stones
hard and smooth to the touch.
He scraped them clear of all earth,
scoured their surfaces, sluiced them
with water again and yet again
until they shone, until they were beautiful,
scorched them in a careful fire
of shaved samaan and jasmine leaves,
burnt them in this small fire,
held fast to them when they cooled.

He walked twenty miles carrying the stones,
stones of water, stones of flame,
forever beautiful, holy, true, and strong.
At Parika he took a slim boat, slid
with a dark ferryman up far Essequibo,
came to a place of ancient suns,
where the river makes a dancing pool,
the forest's thick, and rare birds sing.
The stones like silvery plums
he offers to the Gods with courtesy,
lays them exactly in the hunting pattern
he would have taught his son to use.

Cold! He found the heavens cold!
Never will the fresh shoots by the river spring,
the winds whispering, the moon cascading down.
Thick tears brim the circles of his eyes,
the salt of horror clogs his throat.
Though breath was sweet and beauty all around,
nothing that makes a difference ever can take place —
no sense in anything, the emptiness that waits.
He knows his fate, the endless fate of man,
no matter what creation he perfects
never to reach a limit to his longing
never to find a meaning for his loss
never to get the attention of the stars
shining beyond the end of their own ending.

TREE OF DREAMS

I went out and bought a cabbage for supper.
Fire shone in the night.
We bad-talked Dolores and her brood
then I climbed in my tree of dreams.
I got up early and went to work as usual:
golden decisions, morsels of wisdom all day.
At home the left-overs are thrown out
and for all eternity evil is redressed.

MASSA DAY DONE

Viv in a mood today, you only have to watch,
see the jaw grinding, he stabbing the pitch, back-lift big.
Look how he stare down the wicket, spear in he eye,
he going to start sudden, violent, a thunder shock.
Man, this could be an innings! This could make life good.

You see how he coming in, how he shoulder relax,
how he spin the bat, how he look up at the sun,
how he seem to breathe deep, how he swing the bat, swing,
how he look around like a lord, how he chest expan'.
You ever see the man wear helmet? Tell me?
They say he too proud an' foolish.
Nah! He know he worth, boy;
the bowler should wear helmet, not he.
Remember long this day, holy to be here.
See him stalk the high altar o' the mornin' air.

You ever see such mastery in this world?
You ever see a man who dominate so?
This man don't know forbearance,
he don't know surrender or forgive,
he lash the ball like something anger him.
Look how the man torment today!
He holding the bat, it could be a axe.
Look how he grinding he jaw again, boy,
how he head hold cock an' high
and he smile, he gleam, like a jaguar.
Don't bring no flighty finery here; it gone!
Bring the mightiest man, Viv husk he.
He always so, he stay best fo' the best.

I tell you, he smile like he hungry;
you ever see this man caress?

That mood hold he, it bite he!
He pound the ball, look at that, aha!
Like he vex, he slash, he pull, he hook,
he blast a way through the cover, man,
he hoist the ball like cannon ball
gone far and wild, scattering the enemy,
and foe turn tremble, danger all about.
It's butchery today; bat spill blood
and he cut like he cutting hog on a block;
nobody could stop he in that mood.

Almighty love be there! Almighty love, boy.
We know from the start, he one o' we.
Something hurt he bad, you could see,
as if heself alone could end we slavery!

Which book will I find you browsing in?
'There', you will say, finding the page,
as if no time had passed at all
to wear away life's bright-edged blade a little more.
'When Isaac Singer died he said,
"What the earth swallows is soon forgotten".
Wrong. "Like moonlight on whitest sand
we use that dark to gleam, to shimmer".'

Following a plough through ancient fields
we turn up treasures:
sun-varnished plums that sweeten to the taste.
A Cypriot proverb:
our history is a black stone carved with wings.
Swords shine in Agamemnon's cupboard:
a traveller's fire lit by Gibbon's noble prose.

Still virgin, Newton died at eighty-five.
Was it worth it to discover
the laws of all the universe?
Ah, we have long loved books together
but Walcott's Homer says it well:
'A girl smells better than a book'.
No, the poet stands himself corrected,
'A girl smells better than whole libraries'.

We have gone long ways apart.
After ferocious evil in the gentle land –
throats gashed to make second mouths of screams,
eyes coldly savaged out of still-fleshed skulls
(Oh, what a work of hate is man!) –
snowfall in Kathmandu;
in that far world where mountains climb
gleaming, that age-old, god-filled bastion,
you're safe with love and books and the high stars.

A world away in dark, dazed Guyana,
I settle for the comfortableness of love,
a good wife's caring, the miracle of sons,
a sea-wind murmuring in green trees.
There's well-drawn tea on the veranda,
delicious meat patties melting on the tongue,
jobs to do for money, men from Porlock –
the poetry later, should there still be time.

Let us choose together the spirit's victories:
Mandlestam's widow counting out like gold
word by word his poems in her head –
'The strength of men against cruelty and power
is memory's victory over man's forgetting';
and wisdom's final lesson, and most true –
'He only merits freedom, merits life,
who daily has to conquer them anew.'

You told me once:
'We think we are immortal
And we are.' It is so still.
Truth does not die and we have savoured it.
The morning's beauty lasts for all its time.

What shall I say, old friend?
Distance, time, still brings no rift.
We sail our separate seas
but when the sea tracks cross
the bright sails unfurled still flash
as I remember, and feel no loss;
the lines that tighten round the mooring post
are strong and taut against the ocean's drift.

THE WEATHER IN SHANTY TOWN

The poets sing, the sweet words gleam like shining laces:
'When the sun harnesses the earth like a goldsmith,
praise the rain, praise the cold lady rain!
When the black storm throws pelting rain down in spears,
praise the fire of the sun, praise the gold wand of the sun!
This land is land of big weathers, black and gold;
storms and fierce heat descend like cruel princes,
black warlords in their thunder palaces.
Under the new moon sometimes there is peace of weather,
rain falling like white lilies on the iron streets:
praise, praise the convenor of the dark winds, the bright airs!'

No poets' words for shanty town: the weather kills and cankers every day.
The black storm in the morning shakes the tilting huts.
Women stuff the cracked walls full with rags against the pour of rain.
Their children play in drowning pools, laughing in the sudden mud.
The black rain and the flail of storm is horrible:
the sodden damp stinking, cess pits overflowing, dryness nowhere.
The water pearls on black tin walls in sweating dews of filth.
The wet air swims like slime in every space and lung.
The rain is piss in shanty town, it brings no grace of silver.

Another day the avid sun hammers the hard earth gold.
Flies blacken the silver eyes of dead pigs in the dumping grounds.
Dust stuffs the bright air streaming from the sky.
It is hot as ovens, hot as engines, hot as deserts.
The heat simmers, the sun sings in the air, torpor everywhere.
The scums of old rain crack like scabs on beggars' sores.
The brass of sunlight poisons shanty town, the hot air fumes with shame.
The smell rises in a shimmering fog, a smell of death and guts.
Black vultures land with dusty wings to browse on heated filth;
the children blaze with joy and race to catch them on the carrion grounds.

Men in good clothes do not feel the weather.
Men sweet with food do not fear the weather.
Men in shining cars glide easy through all weather.
Paper-mighty men at desks do not hate the weather.
Men in strong houses do not know the weather of this world.
Such men, such cocooned men, they do not live in shanty town.
The weather in their hearts is mild, they have not lived in shanty town.
In shanty town the anger hangs like smoke, like fire.
The weather in those hearts is storm, the weather in those hearts is hate.

ON READING BIOGRAPHIES OF ROBERT LOWELL, SYLVIA PLATH, JOHN BERRYMAN AND ANNE SEXTON IN RAPID SUCCESSION

I see there is not much to tell
in a life if it goes well,
but it goes bad, well then, hooray,
there is always much to say.
Hideous lives these great ones live:
forever take, and never give –
but then allowance must be given
to the soul that's sick and driven.
Cruel fighting, knives unsheathed,
thorns around the laurels wreathed;
desperate loves, antic madness,
fits of ecstasy 'midst sadness;
moods and alcoholic tantrums,
the boom and bash of beaten drums
sounding out the loud despairs
of re-reiterated fears.
Descents repeated into Hell
where agony and anguish dwell
is the story of their lives:
art on madness ever thrives.
Self-flagellating lash and groan
lend a rich compelling tone
to each self-exculpating tale
and every self-confessing wail.
Others, of course, have lives as well
and didn't volunteer for hell:
no matter, the non-creative other,
be it spouse, or child, or mother,
or friend, or lover, who had the luck
to touch or even chance to be in suck-
ing distance of that heroic taint

enrols to play the willing role of saint
and put up with each desperate trick,
accept in full what's deeply sick,
issuing from the one appointed
from on high, the Muse-anointed.
It matters not what others bear —
the poet's duty is quite clear,
the lesson is as plain as day:
'Let others suffer, I go my way
in fulfillment of the Olympian plot:
The work's important, lives are not.'

Or, not to make such a song and dance about it:

God save you, should you cross the path
of Robert Lowell or Sylvia Plath.

THE PEAR-WOOD CUP

Carved pear-wood:
golden as if filled with sun,
cleaned to a shone perfection,
handled to fit a big and battered knuckle,
simple, ordinary, well-proportioned shape,
deep-bowled for a deep thirstiness.
In it the deep, long wear of usefulness,
entering, lasting, then transforming,
has engraved a beauty without passion:
there is no harm in this good thing.
The man who made it lived when times were slow,
knew old occupations that start at morning light.
This cup has no comparison,
no others match it on the kitchen shelf.
In it the touch of generations
joins the taste of everyday:
cold, clear water gets colder, clearer.
The trouble is with us:
too few good things kept safe
come down from the ancestors
to teach us what is past and prized.

GIFTS FOR A FAREWELL

Koetsu, famous for his tea-bowls,
mainly black, others rufous or turkey-wattle red,
some splashed with white as from an eagle's droppings:
his glazing holds a brightness like fireflies.
Eighteen tea-bowls that he made are left.
All the rest are gone, thousands they say;
the centuries have stamped them all to pieces.
I wish you this gift, a bowl so baked and spun.

Farmers in vivid scarlet clothes
till strawberry fields in Pougastel.
A wild wind haunts that Breton coast
where fish-boats bring in their silver catch.
Honoured for beauty, I have read,
you must walk in Pougastel.

In Mexico the Tarascans long ago
made mosaics from the wings of birds.
Most famous of all villages in this art
Tzintzuntzan on a golden lake –
in Mayan meaning 'tresses of the day-star'.
They worked thus: drop by drop an orchid's glue
bound gold-green feathers into tapestry.
May you seek and love such wonders all your life.

These gifts for you, Philip O'Meara,
friend of the good hours, you would like to know
these things and you will treasure them
and yet reflect how simply beauty falls
and the dark comes and hearts slow.
You who dance upon the ice
have always known what dwells below.

POEM

(for Arthur Seymour)

One night your poems were in my hands
when sudden as blindness in the dark
the lamplight in the room went out
and I was sightless in the poem's heart.
I sat there in the deepening night
your poems held upon my knees;
the sea-wind made its quiet sound,
a half-moon slowly etched the trees.
In my mind their cadence grew
like waves that run against a far-off shore,
that restless whisper from the world begun,
that eternal sound men have hungered for.

CANDLESTICK MAKER

Beneath the ox-tail, shit bubbles and descends;
peasant fare, smell of cake-stalls in the air.
At last he wakes, bolt-straight,
eyes afire, from his complex sleep,
throws off the embroidered heavy clothes,
sets about the task, self-given;
matches the multiplying suns,
the green glaze of leaves, the Plato cave,
the bears, the waterfall, the galleries of love.
He makes the single candlestick
golden, polished, perfect, sure;
sets in it one perfect candle
and lights it to light the world.
Though the taper's frail
and the wind a-howl,
full of the hiss of serpents,
blows the flame flat
and the flame flutters, fails,
nothing can be put out again,
far darkness is illumined.
The candlestick maker:
ah, his craft is needed.
Nothing ceases when he begins
the sift and seethe of endless time;
light will last forever now
radiance in every tumbled grave.

BETWEEN SILENCE AND SILENCE
THERE SHOULD BE ONLY PRAISE

Should there be a great flood
whole cities would be cast on the fierce water,
floating, drifting, down to an ancient sea;
men and women shouting at the windows,
carrying children to the rooftops,
whimpering in the bleak wind's fury.
Desperate swimming as the houses sink;
life's comfortable arrangements awry and lost.
That slender-waisted girl, sure of her beauty,
she is gone too, with the despots and clowns.
Under the vast sky, much pointless activity –
as well a skull pick its nose and snort
to breathe the evening air.

On the black creek a man's at work;
a fisherman sets a nest of ants afloat,
clump of twigs and green leaves clotted
so intricately to make this insect home,
neat, entangled, well-planned habitation,
now, suddenly adrift, the ant-swarm circles,
tests the water's edge, retreats,
all safety ended.

The impassive fisher sits above;
the floating nest, his subtle bait,
spills ants amidst the swirling flood;
fish flash, gather for the living feast.
He takes his time to flick the rod
assured of victims as the ants drop off
the sinking nest, efficient lure.
The ants' nest drowns and sinks
and bubbles rise like pearls and burst.

Man need not have been. No one knows why
God maintains his kingdom without persuasion:
the dark world of the forest and the river stirs,
intricate catacomb, the grub-furrow under earth
leading to stone, the sun-soar over clouds,
mud caked Johnny Smallfoot, the bent idiot,
whose pleasant laughter maddens those who sorely hurt him.
Shadows pass, empires are cast down.
Friend, it is past the time when tears matter:
between silence and silence, there should be only praise.

About the Author

Ian McDonald was born in Trinidad in 1933. After attending school in Port of Spain he went to university in Cambridge to read History. In 1955, he went to Guyana where he has lived ever since.

Born into a white West Indian family, Ian McDonald has led a varied life. Initially working with Bookers Ltd (owners of Guyana's sugar estates), he continued working with the nationalised Guyana Sugar Corporation, and was for many years its Administrative Director. He has written for the Guyanese national press, and with his friend A.J. Seymour, he worked to revive the journal, *Kyk-over-Al*, which he continues to edit. In recent years, he has been a key figure in Guyana's Cultural Commission. McDonald's own writing career began in the 1950s with publications of his poetry in anthologies and journals such as *Bim*. He went on to write plays and a novel, *The Hummingbird Tree*, which has subsequently been made into a BBC film. His previous poetry collections include *Mercy Ward* (1988), *Essequibo* (1992) and *Jaffo the Calypsonian* (Peepal Tree, 1994).

Ian McDonald was recently awarded a richly deserved Honorary PhD by the University of the West Indies.

Also by Ian McDonald

jaffo the calypsonian   ISBN 0 948833 65 3, 1994, £6.95

Ian McDonald's poetry embraces Caribbean possibility with a romantic fervour which still acknowledges what is harsh and painful in the region. He has both the gift to see 'the ibis-bird in pigeons' and an ironical consciousness of the poet's gilding eye. There are love poems of lyric grace and stunning simplicity; exuberant paeans to nature in all its beauty, fierceness and cruelty; narratives which grip and characters who are powerfully memorable. Here is a celebration of life which is made all the more intense by the consciousness of mortality which lurks behind every vivid occasion.

Visit the Peepal Tree website & buy books online at:

www.peepaltreepress.com